Pearls and Lace

Pearls
and
Lace

STACIE ALLEN

PEARLS AND LACE

iUniverse books may be ordered through booksellers or by contacting:

iUniverse
1663 Liberty Drive
Bloomington, IN 47403
www.iuniverse.com
844-349-9409

ISBN: 978-1-6632-0523-0 (sc)
ISBN: 978-1-6632-0522-3 (e)

Library of Congress Control Number: 2020913084

Print information available on the last page.

iUniverse rev. date: 08/11/2020

Emotions about Writing This Book
I thought of this long ago. I hope I
will—I'm sure to take flight.
Something that I love to do, paint,
shop, be creative, and write,
Letting others in the realms of my head.
What will they say, I'm cuckoo, strange, a bit crazy?
"Maybe her mind is just dead!"
"I like it! I learned from it! I love every word she said!"
We've all been there before. Family,
friends, someone I know for sure.
I'm writing this book so all can see.
Happy, sad, aroused, on the brink of going mad.
I'm anxious, a bit fearful. I'm ready.
Must put my words to the test.
Stop thinking so negatively; put those silly thoughts to rest.
So as you turn the pages, I think you
should know that every little poem
Has a story to show.
Enjoy.

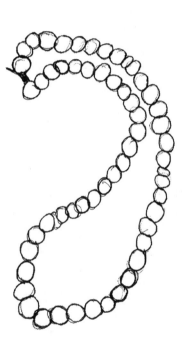

Strands, shiny, imperfect.
See-through surface.
Drifting.
What's your purpose?
Lights of royalty.
Learn yourself.
Simple pearls wrapped in lace,
Uncovering, balancing, discovering,
Seeking a higher place.

Body has the shakes,
Heart pounding.
Earthquakes.
Surroundings vanished.
Bright sun, flowers covering my feet.
Frost begins to heat.
Inner self began a healing.
Eyes met. Nothing else matters.
Wet is dry; dry is drip.
Broken; now fixed.
The first time my eyes saw you,
Shining stars.
At this moment, truly divine.
Only you and I.
Love.

Zesty
Lover and bestie,
Lasting all night.
Feeling sexy, he takes his time, rubs his body.
Tongue, hands, feet. Lover has special skills
That no supplementary can beat.
Makes me feel zesty.
Bodies twirling to R. Kelly.
Oh, my thighs. Lover is always on the rise.
Keeps me a-drip all night.
Memorable.
Levers you right.
My bestie.

Pearls
and
Lace

Explosion
My body is glowing just right.
Spraying on my Juicy Couture.
Wearing black lace, nothing more.
It's about to be an explosion.
It's about to be an explosion.
Running my hands down your back.
I love it when you lay your head upon my lap.
Yes, I'm giving you a fatal erection.
Ooh yes, come, baby; start that injection.
It's about to be an explosion.
It's about to be an explosion.
My hands are gripping you tight.
It's grand to be thumping all through the night.
Legs pushed back. Give it to me, baby. I need an attack.
Oh, a six-pack.
Pull me closer.
It's about to be an explosion.

Friend of Mine

Friends from the start, we share. We play. We love.
Friends care.
I would do anything for you, and you
would do anything for me.
I respect you, would never neglect you.
You're my friend I can trust.
Okay, what happened?
Now there's a man you claim to desire.
The man you speak of sets my soul on fire,
Belongs to me.
Now I see:
You took him from me.
What happened to us? What about we?
What about trust?
Dear friend of mine, no more do I see
One lonely pearl.
It's all about me.

Got Rid of You

Feeling great this morning. Slept the whole night through.
Got rid of some drama. Got rid of you.
Cleaned the house when you left.
Turned the music up loud.
Pranced naked in my living room, feeling calm, shining,
So proud of myself that I got rid of you.
Poured a glass of wine. Bathwater for one.
Bath full of bubbles, so soft, so smooth.
Got rid of my man.
I can do it alone.
I make good money; my body is toned.
I'm feeling great this morning,
Smiling all the way to work.
Can't wait to go home.
I do what I do, and I'm doing it alone.

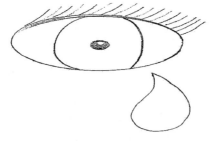

I Cried

Sitting, staring, lonely inside.
It's hard to crack a pearl inside.
Easier to hide.
I cried. I cried.
Lost a soul so close,
Known all my life.
I cried. I cried.
Tears
I cried and didn't want anyone to see.
Reminders all around.
I cried. I cried.
Time has stopped.
I miss you. I need you.
I cried. I cried.
You were my pillar.
My life has dropped.
I cried.

The Hoover Song

Sweet, sexy female, looks to be in her thirties,
fair skin, long hair, and a body like Beyoncé's,
living with a man, supposedly her fiancé.
This man is sort of like a sweeper. See, she pays the
bills. She takes him to dinner. She owns the car. This
man gives her no love. When he does, it's superfast.
Chorus: The woman has a man known as a Hoover: no
job, no direction. Drains her affection. He is a Hoover,
a straight Hoover, sweetie. The man's a Hoover.
She buys what he sips, gives him money daily.
And what does he do? Suck all the gravy.
Chorus: The woman has a man known as a Hoover: no
job, no direction. Drains her affection. He is a Hoover,
a straight Hoover, sweetie. Your man's a Hoover.
She works two jobs just to pay the rent.
Not one dime has this man spent.
Chorus: The woman has a man known as a Hoover: no
job, no direction. Drains her affection. He is a Hoover,
a straight Hoover. Sweetie, your man's a Hoover.
This man is a sweeper, just dusty all day.
Chorus: The woman has a man known as a Hoover: no
job, no direction. Drains her affection. He is a Hoover,
a straight Hoover. Sweetie, the man's a Hoover.
Repeat chorus.

Pearls
and
Lace

Stumbled out of bed. Uneasy night.
Staring out the kitchen window,
looking at the morning sun.
Placing a pot on the stove, I began to cook.
Suddenly my body shook.
Thrown to the floor; kicked in the chest.
I wish I were invisible.
I wish I could hide.
Problems, as you can see.
I love him so much; it's deep in my core.
I want to help him. Don't think I can take it
No more.
Drinking, fighting, crying.
Where is the laughter?
Police knocking at the door.
Took you away. It's over. No more.
The next day,
Morning sun, I jump from my bed.
I slept like a baby.
Coffee in hand; smile on my face.
I love my life. Now it's a peaceful place.

That woman's not like me; can't you see?
Her! Next to you. She is not like me.
She wants your business; please understand.
We together favor sky, the land.
Blinded by body.
Keep in perspective, this is my space
She wants to taste.
The woman, you see, is not like me.
Stop sleeping in darkness.
Just wake up and see.

Done

Shutting me down every time I have something to say.
Done.
No more closing the door, looking the other way.
Done.
Declining you on this day.
Surely, I've said this before.
I'm done, you see.
You and I are no more.
Done.
Smiling all the time, not taking me seriously.
Thoughts all figured out.
No fun, trust, or love.
I'm done.
Not with me.
You should proceed to the door.
I'm done.

Pearls

and

Lace

I Made a Mistake

Can't shake how I'm feeling.
Don't want to go on this way—
Racing thoughts,
Mushy body.
No swallowing, no sleep.
I wish I could take it all back.
Insecurities felt.
Meaningless arguments.
I made a mistake;
Thought about it all night.
Unfamiliar bed.
Come back. Don't take that flight.
Just one mistake
Put the pearls in place.
Your touch, your smell.
I made a mistake.
Let's not end this way.
I made a mistake.

It Hurts Inside
I can't stop crying.
It hurts inside.
You left way too soon.
It hurts inside.
I'm alone,
Motionless,
Numb.
You should be near me.
It hurts inside.
Craving you.
I don't understand;
We were together from the start.
Now my life is ripped apart.
It hurts inside.
Hard to go on this way.
Memories of you and the words you would say.

Pearls
and
Lace

I think of you.
Many times I cry, I do.
I miss your smile, your touch.
I cry, yes, I do.
Our talks, our walks.
What I would give to see your face.
You're a soul no one can replace,
Yet you're in a better place,
No anguish, no hurt,
Observing me.
Blue skies, clouds, and rain.
The love we shared will never fade.
The joy you gave, heaven-made.
Press harder. Move stronger.
Live life. Make it grand.
But still I cry.
For you, my love, I will not let life pass me by.
I know this is what you want,
Yet I still cry.

Yes Girl

Yes, I'll do it. Leave it for me. Yes. Why not?

I'm the yes girl, giving you what you need,

Always trying to please.

Yes, what else can I do?

I'm the yes girl, and I'll say yes just for you.

Whatever you ask, I'll never say no.

I don't know how to.

So, it's yes for all.

I wake up every morning to say yes all day.

Why? What did you think?

What else would I say?

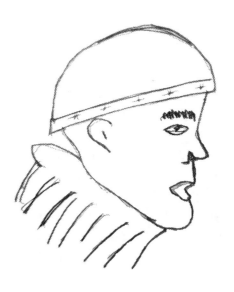

Dysfunctional

I love the way you smell, the way you walk,
Your smile, your kiss,
The way you talk.
Every time I'm around you,
I get dysfunctional. I get dysfunctional.
The color of your hair, the glow on your skin,
The dimple in your cheek, the curve of your chin.
I get dysfunctional. I get dysfunctional.
Your touch, your body,
The sparkle in your eyes.
I get dysfunctional. I get dysfunctional.
I'm telling you the best way I know how:
I love you.

Shine Song

Everybody raise your hands and look straight to the sky.
Give the one and only. Let the Lord see your shine.
Woke up this morning, feet on the ground.
I looked straight to the sky and let the Lord see my shine.
Energizing sun, children having fun.
Let him see you praise.
No matter your story,
Always remember to let him see you shine,
Always giving glory.
Just shine.

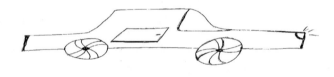

Parking Lot Shenanigans
Mr. Dark, Mr. Driven,
Staring straight down my shirt.
He says, "Now this is livin'."
My view is his belt.
Well, his pants came undone and dropped to the ground.
Gripping him tight as my lips start to round.
This man is so wide. Along the sides back and forth,
He started to glide.
Down my throat.
So intense, so enjoyable.
Parking lot. Do we care?
Okay, the rocket blows. Down my boobs it goes.
What just happened? What did I do?
Mr. Tall, Dark, and Driven,
I really don't know you.

Pearls
and
Lace

A Lump in the Air
Not talking. Nothing to share.
On your phone,
The computer.
Lacking communication,
Intimacy.
Why are you here?
Thinking of the past more frequently.
We used to be the pair.
The relationship is over; I wish you could see.
The worst feeling is having a lump in the air.
No thoughts. So unfair.
Time to move on. Don't be afraid.
More closet space. No more time you should waste.
Please go on;
Stop taking up space.

Pearls and Lace

Racing thoughts all day and all night.
Can't take my mind off a hideous sight.
My past is most grim.
Lacking a smile, kept deeply within.
Come with me to a place no one else would go.
Hurry, together.
Let me help. Please follow.
Did not like the sight.
Visuals keeping me up, frightened all night.

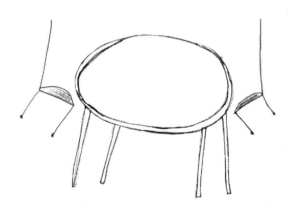

Man across the table, so scary, so big.
Why the invite?
Was it something I said?
You look at me strangely
With your big ugly hat.
You don't get the message: not interested.
Respect your wife, the vows you said.
I should have told your wife long ago.
Stop calling my phone,
Sending flowers.
Just stop.
I wish she had not married so low.

Pearls
and
Lace

Running up the hill,
Only to fall back down.
Get back up before I hit bottom.
Don't let go.
Must push and climb.
Don't want others to see me fall.
Keep hitting the big brick wall.
Viewing a way to make a crack.
Making my way to the top.
I will be back.

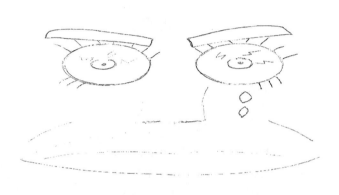

Green-eyed monster,
Not pretty at all,
Brings you down,
Makes you look small.
Glaring and staring,
Checking everything I do.
You're not getting any sleep.
Please find something for you.
Stop wanting to be me.
Just stay in your lane.
Don't let this color
Destroy your name.

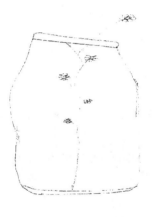

The prettiest, tallest flower in the bunch
Keeps her petals so very low,
Not happy at all.
But the rest of the bunch is standing tall.
Other strong flowers begin to approach.
She moves to the back,
While others like to be seen.
Not understanding why the stronger ones adore.
Stop, pretty flower. Stop being insecure.

Pearls

and

Lace

Sinking so low,
All I see is the dark.
I see guns. I see bullets and blood. I can't cope.
Balled up as a fetus,
I don't want to move.
Say nothing to me.
Please don't look my way.
I pray that tomorrow brings me a better day.

Pearls
and
Lace

You really think so highly of me.
You anxiously ask me to come see.
Well, I'm busy.
You're not taking no for an answer.
I go.
I stop what I'm doing, and what happens to me?
Nothing to see but a room with plastic sheets.
Noticing quickly that it's a trap.
Almost lost my life.
Trust from me? Never again. That's a wrap.

Pearls
and
Lace

Living on High
You can't take me low.
All the things you did to me
On my face will never show.
So far above you,
Places you're not programmed to go.
Surrounded myself with go-getters and pros.
Move on.
Losers, nobodies, haters, average joes.
Time to let go.

We women have power.
We have poise.
We were born with it.
Winking my eye.
Crossing my legs.
Painted toes.
Full lips.
We women have power.
Tossing my hair.
We women have power,
But we love hard and we take care.

Trying to be the best version of me,
True to myself. That's all I can be.
Exercising, staying healthy,
Juggling family,
Climbing the ladder of success,
Working tirelessly,
Saving money,
Drinking water,
Engaging in relaxation techniques,
Keeping up with friends,
Praying for love and peace,
Supporting those who need,
Faithfully being the best version of me.

Pearls and Lace

Blaming You
Extra weight?
Blaming you.
No job?
Blaming you.
No friends?
Blaming you.
I hate where I live.
Blaming you.
I cut my hair.
Blaming you.
The decisions I made.
What did I say?
Who did you blame?

Pearls
and
Lace

Telling everyone that you're my friend,
My sister, my love, always till the end.
But the real you is slick and sly.
I saw you the other night with a man I used to date.
You're calling my friends, telling them I'm fake.
I used to love you, would do anything for you,
But the real you is slick and sly,
Calling my sister, looking for information,
Dressing like me. The craziness must stop.
Telling coworkers my secrets, my thoughts.
But the real you is so slick and sly.
I can't take the stickiness, so it's goodbye.

Cracks and wrinkles, dots, blemishes,
all around my nose.
Mirror, mirror,
Nothing is the same,
And anything goes
Only for the night.
Never been seen in the light.

Pearls and Lace

Darling, please don't open your mouth.
I don't want to listen to anything you say.
Don't care what you did all day.
I sit back on the couch.
Let me rest my feet.
Quiet; don't move.
I have something to say,
More interesting, delightful,
In my head all day.
Don't interrupt.
Just listen.

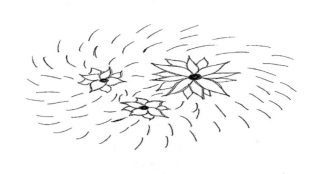

Unbothered
You know what you did.
Brushed off my shoulders.
It's getting old.
Unbothered.
Never touch my soul.
Keep far away.
Distance is the best.
Unbothered.

Pearls and Lace

Stop the copying.
Stop the following.
Stop repeating what I say.
We are not the same.
Stop copying me.
Stop copying me.
I say magic words in week one.
Week two, they become yours.
Stop the following.
Stop repeating what I say.
We are not the same.
Stop copying me.
Stop copying me.
I like blue ice cream.
Then you say you do too.
I sleep with the light on.
You say you do too.
I like black roses.
You say you do too.
Stop copying me.
We are not the same.

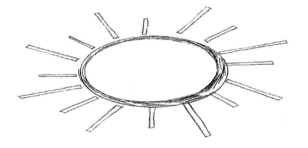

Head of my space, my domain, my face.
I have control. Everything is organized in one place.
Thoughts, finances, happy and not in a box.
Moving to one drum, I am woman.
I'm self-made; this is not fiction.
My grind keeps improving. I'm at the top of the game.
Other people, so lame. Not bragging.
Reading all the lines and people left behind.
Deceiving souls spitting out of my pores.
My wounds, my sores, head of space,
A happy or a lonely place.

Pearls
and
Lace

Handsome imposter,
I've seen the facts in six weeks.
You can't keep it up.
Be yourself.
Stop making people up.

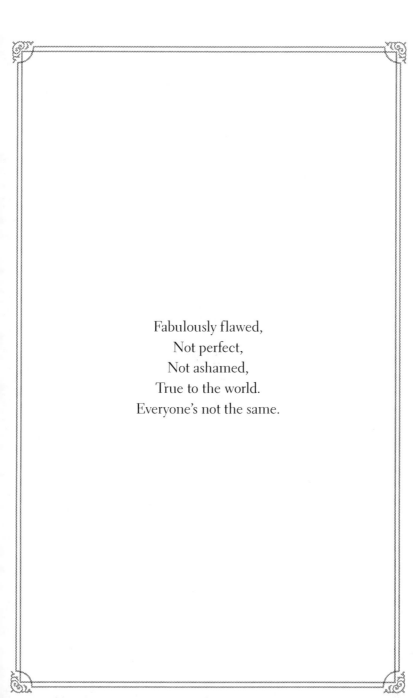

Fabulously flawed,
Not perfect,
Not ashamed,
True to the world.
Everyone's not the same.

He is all business,
No knocking him down.
Bet he has a woman
With pearls in her crown.

Pearls
and
Lace

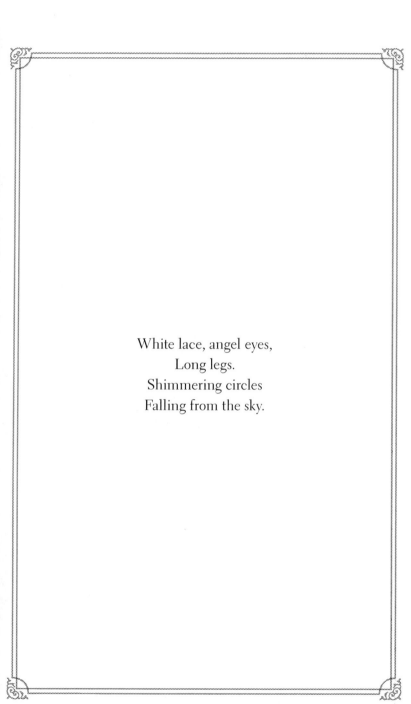

White lace, angel eyes,
Long legs.
Shimmering circles
Falling from the sky.

Pearls
and
Lace

Did he notice me?
I made quite an entrance.
I fell and lost my glasses.
Embarrassed. Should I hide?
He's looking this way.
Let me take him for a ride.

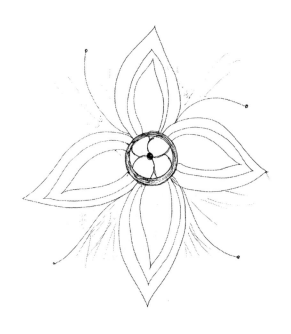

Let me take you on this journey.
Little girl loved pearls,
Hid them in lace.
Frightened, always in forbidden space.
Covering my face.
Baggy clothes.
Wish no one noticed.
But so hard to hide.

Pearls

and

Lace

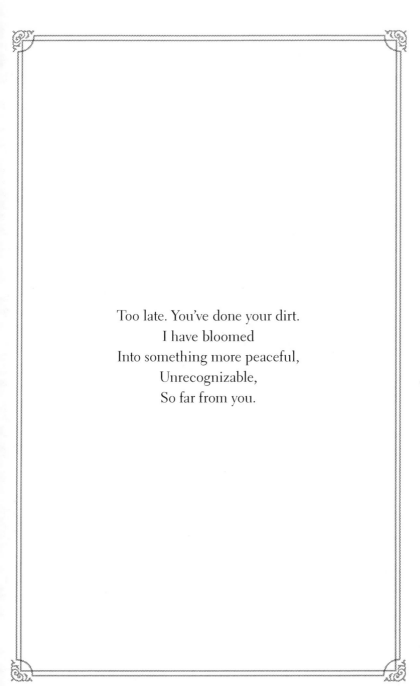

Too late. You've done your dirt.
I have bloomed
Into something more peaceful,
Unrecognizable,
So far from you.

Pearls and Lace

Every time I meet someone new,
White picket fence, large house, kids.
Who knew?
Educated, beautiful,
But distorted. So true.
Get it together; everyone is not for you.

Printed in the United States
By Bookmasters